PRESENTED TO

BY

_____

RICH DeVOS

FROM MY HEART

10

Lessons for Life

J. Countryman
Nashville, Tennessee

This book is dedicated to the people who give me hope

*and love me and have helped me when
life was slowing me down. They have all been there,
in person and in prayer:*

Helen, my wife of forty-seven years;

Our children and their spouses:
Dick and Betsy, Dan and Pam, Cheri and Bob, Doug and Maria;

Our grandchildren:
Rick, Elissa, Andrea, and Ryan (Dick and Betsy's children);
Cassandra, Sydney, and Cole (Dan and Pam's children);
Hannah, Katelyn, Benjamin, and Jessa (Cheri and Bob's children); and
Dalton, Micaela, Monreau, and Olivia (Doug and Maria's children);

Plus untold others who have prayed for me.

"An exemplary little book by an exemplary human being. He ends by telling us that it was required of him that he show a will to live: He did, and lives on, to our benefit."

—WILLIAM F. BUCKLEY JR., best-selling author of *God and Man at Yale, Saving the Queen, Stained Glass,* and *Overdrive*

"A compelling testimony of a remarkable man's life journey filled with hope and faith. I loved the book!"

—JERRY COLANGELO, Owner, NBA Phoenix Suns

"Rich DeVos, one of the wisest men I've known, dispenses that wisdom powerfully in Hope from My Heart. *I heartily recommend it; it is filled with great lessons for life."*

—CHARLES W. COLSON, Prison Fellowship Ministries

"What an inspiring, wise, life-changing book! These pages share powerful lessons, transforming moments, and personal epiphanies—all inviting us to re-examine this precious gift we call life."

—DR. STEPHEN R. COVEY, best-selling author of *The Seven Habits of Highly Effective People*

*"*Hope from My Heart: 10 Lessons for Life *challenged me to assess my personal value chart for accuracy and current relativity."*

—JULIUS ERVING, Member, NBA Hall of Fame

"This book is an instructive and inspirational guide to the principles that enabled Rich DeVos to become an extraordinary entrepreneur and a national leader in building an America where freedom, faith, and family flourish."

—EDWIN J. FEULNER, President, The Heritage Foundation

"It is fun; it is enlightening, and inspirational. A great read."

—BETTY FORD, former First Lady of the United States

"This goal-oriented man of power, fame, and wealth reveals the Source of the values that sustained and empowered him. I plan to give this book to 550 world leaders in a score of nations."

—JOHN EDMUND HAGGAI, Founder and Chairman, Haggai Institute

"Americans need this book for inspiration, for encouragement—and as a how-to book for making the American-ism all that it can be."

—PAUL HARVEY, Host, *Paul Harvey News*

"This book is one of the most interesting and compelling stories I have ever read. I can safely and honestly say it is bound to touch the souls of all who read it."

—RICHARD HAYMAN, Principal Arranger of The Boston Pops Orchestra

CONTENTS

ACKNOWLEDGEMENTS

There are many people who helped me write this book, and I want to thank them from the bottom of my heart. My deepest gratitude goes to Helen, my dear wife, who shared many of the experiences I've written about in this book. She made many valuable contributions and played an important editing role.

I also wish to thank several others who contributed to this book in various ways: our children—Dick, Dan, Cheri, and Doug, Dr. Paul Conn, Ken Ross, Judith Markham, Kim Bruyn, Billy Zeoli, Bill Payne, Alan Nevins, and the many wonderful people at the J. Countryman division of Thomas Nelson Publishers.

Just as I hope this book is a blessing to those who read it, I've been truly blessed by Helen and the many others who helped me write it.

PREFACE

This is a book of practical wisdom, filled with many of the simple insights I have gained throughout my own seventy-plus years of life experiences. My goal in sharing the wisdom I've gained through experience—both good and bad—is to give you hope in *your* life.

Patrick Henry once said, "I have but one lamp by which my feet are guided, and that is the lamp of experience. I know of no way of judging of the future but by the past." Because I personally have learned the truth of these words, I want to offer you the benefit of the light from my own lamp of experience. I want to impart hope from my heart.

I am a practical man. Much of my experience has been based on common sense, intuition, observation, and inherited values. I have always enjoyed learning by doing, and in the doing, I have made my share of mistakes. But most of the time, by the grace of God, I have managed to succeed. I am incurably optimistic, sometimes naïve, dogged in my determination, and undeterred by defeat. I learned long ago that hope, even when it seems unwarranted, irrational, or reckless to others, is essential in life and a prerequisite to success. One of the most powerful forces in the world is the will of men and women who believe in themselves, who dare to hope and aim high, who go confidently after the things they want from life.

And when I talk about success, I am not just measuring it by money or position. In fact, I believe success is using the talents that God has given you to the best of your ability. People are individuals created by God, and I have devoted much of my life to promoting the positive values and character traits that enable those individuals to achieve personal and financial success. I believe that it is always more powerful to live out your values than to preach them. Often when people ask how I became successful, I reply, "I just went to work every day, did the best I could to advance the cause, and trusted God." And I never lost hope—in my dreams, in other people, and, above all, in my God.

Experience is the best teacher. I've learned this over and over again throughout my life. And it was brought home vividly to me three years ago, at age seventy, when I had a heart transplant. You cannot go through the experience of a heart transplant—and survive physically, psychologically, and spiritually—without a deep examination, or re-examination, of what is important in life. My heart transplant tested the strength of my own personal faith and values. I hope you never have to go through a similar experience, and statistically very few of you will, but sooner or later, every one of you will face some kind of crisis in your life. When that happens, you need to be prepared. You need to have an unshakeable faith in God as well as the inner resources sufficient to carry you through the worst of times. Most of all, you need to have hope.

Aldous Huxley once wrote, "Experience is not what happens to you; it is what you do with what happens to you." The events of our lives flow and change; nothing stays the same. But we can build our lives upon the permanent bedrock of our faith, our values, and our character. This foundation determines what we will do with those changing events.

In the following chapters, I will share with you ten lessons for life, revolving around those philosophies, beliefs, values, and character traits that have proven to be the most sustaining and valuable in my own life. I pray that what I have learned from my own experience will be a lamp of hope as you travel the pathway of your life.

RICH DEVOS
SUMMER 2000

Lesson

1

HOPE

Find rest,

O my soul, in God alone;

my hope comes from him.

PSALM 62:5

Though born of humble beginnings to his parents Simon and Ethel DeVos, Rich DeVos was brought up with strong values and abundant love.

HOPE

No human life is without problems, and I have certainly seen my share. But I have always done my best to view problems as challenges and to never lose hope. I've always believed that a good challenge presents new opportunities—opportunities to learn, to grow, to gain strength, or to reach a higher goal. And I've always believed that the future is in God's hands.

Three years ago, I found myself lying on a gurney in a hospital in a foreign country, being wheeled toward an operating room for a heart transplant. The odds of survival were stacked against me. Up until that moment, I had called the shots for the challenges in my life. I usually set the course. Sink or swim, the responsibility had most often been mine. But this time, I most certainly was not in control.

The very first hint of a problem had appeared almost fourteen years earlier. The day began as any other, but sometime during the morning, I began to feel very unsteady on my feet, as if I were continually losing my balance. I'd bump into doorframes as I exited doorways. Even when I'd set a straight course, I couldn't seem to stop from veering to the left side as I moved.

My wife, Helen, urged me to call the doctor. As my usual optimistic self, I resisted. I was certain that a little rest was all that was necessary to

> *I've always believed that a good challenge presents new opportunities— to learn, to grow, to gain strength, or to reach a higher goal.*

get me back on my feet. But Helen persisted, and I finally agreed.

We were expecting the doctor to prescribe a pill, but instead, he insisted that I immediately check into the hospital for further testing. The final diagnosis was that I had suffered a transient ischemic attack, or TIA, which, the doctors explained, was a warning that a stroke or heart attack was in the making. The doctors advised me to make changes in my lifestyle.

With characteristic determination, I met the problem—the challenge—head-on. I changed my diet, reduced my cholesterol level, and made exercise a part of my daily routine. Also true to character, I resumed my usual hectic schedule of meetings, speaking engagements, and the endless day-to-day details involved in operating Amway with my business partner, Jay Van Andel.

Three years later, on a Fourth of July weekend, our children—Dick, Dan, Cheri, and Doug—and I competed in the Queen's Cup race on our fifty-foot racing sloop, *Windquest.* It was an overnight race across Lake Michigan—from Milwaukee, Wisconsin, to Grand Haven, Michigan. For a pre-race event, we set out in the evening from Grand Haven.

We love the intensity of yacht racing, which requires great physical energy and mental concentration. I was helping with sail changes and spinnaker takedowns when I felt a sharp pain in my chest. I didn't want to worry everyone, so I said nothing about the pain. I just went below and tried to get some rest for the remainder of the night. By the following morning, however, I could no longer ignore the chest pains, and we arranged for a plane to pick me up in Milwaukee and fly me home to Grand Rapids.

In the hospital, a stress test revealed a coronary artery blockage, and Dr. Luis Tomatis, a thoracic surgeon, determined that bypass surgery was necessary.

The last thing I ever expected was to be a candidate for open-heart surgery. Perhaps I'd forgotten about the TIA and the doctor's warning that came with it. Or maybe I was convinced that my healthier diet and exercise routine had solved the problem. At any rate, I was surprised and somewhat discouraged. I found that hope is more difficult to maintain during unexpected challenges.

During surgery, the doctors discovered more arterial damage than they had expected. Instead of bypassing three or four coronary arteries, they operated on six. Nonetheless, the surgery was a success, and the experience gave me a new appreciation of life and new reasons to hope. It also made me more aware of the passage of time. Prior to this, my future had always seemed firmly in place. Suddenly it became less certain. During the recovery process, I learned to relax more, to take more

Although just a novice sailor in his early twenties, Rich DeVos became an expert over the years and competed in many races.

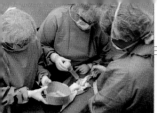

leisure time for myself, and to begin fulfilling some of the dreams Helen and I shared.

Unfortunately, however, my battle with deteriorating health was just beginning. In the summer of 1992, I suffered a stroke. Thankfully, it wasn't terribly severe, but it prompted me to grapple with the difficult question of whether I should continue as president of Amway. I loved the business, and with my partner, Jay, had devoted a large part of my life to nurturing its growth. We had weathered many storms and lived to see the fruits of our labor grow into a large, wonderfully successful company. But I had to ask myself, *Was the daily stress of running a large corporation potentially threatening to my life?* That was a topic I resisted addressing, and a question I certainly didn't want to answer in the affirmative.

I was now on the most healthful diet I had ever eaten in my life, I was exercising regularly, and I was leading a much more leisurely existence. But in spite of all these lifestyle changes, one morning in December, I awoke at about 4:00 A.M. with terrible chest pains. I knew I was having a heart attack.

I was rushed by ambulance to the hospital emergency room, and after I arrived there, my heart almost stopped beating. I remember hearing a nurse in the emergency room counting down my pulse rate. Then I heard her say, "There's no pulse." I don't remember much after that. Mercifully, I passed out.

The doctors managed to revive me, but they were uncertain as to whether I would survive. Dr. Tomatis and Dr. Rick McNamara began talking to my family about an experimental procedure that was being performed at the Cleveland Clinic. They suggested contacting the clinic to see if I could be admitted. When my family inquired about the possibility, the top surgeon at the clinic agreed to examine me, but he wanted everyone to understand that he was making no promises regarding taking me on as a patient. Once again, my hope was buoyed.

My memories of that time are vague, but my oldest son, Dick, remembers that at the clinic, Dr. Cosgrove was rather brusque when I was first wheeled in. He performed his examination, looked at the charts and test results, and then said that he wouldn't make any decisions about taking my case until after he examined me again in the morning. The doctor, who has since become a friend, admitted later that he really didn't expect me to live through the night. The fact that I did was an indication to him that I had a chance, albeit slight, of surviving surgery.

After making sure that we all understood the risks, he agreed to perform bypass surgery.

When you're heading for major surgery or facing a life-threatening situation, you can't avoid wondering if your time is up. That's when you decide whether you're right with God or not.

It was a long procedure, involving three bypasses, and Dr. Cosgrove reported that my heart muscle was severely damaged. My doctors felt confident, however, that my condition would be more stable than it was before the surgery. In hospital-speak, I was in "guarded" condition.

Though weak, I was able to return home in time to celebrate Christmas with my family. The joy was short-lived, however, because I soon developed a staph infection in my chest. In the following weeks, the doctors opened up my chest three more times in their fight to clear up the infection, which had eaten into my ribs, sternum, and the muscle tissue surrounding the incision. I was a mess. Because so much tissue was lost, Dr. Moore, a plastic surgeon, had to cut my pectoral muscles, reposition them, and rebuild my chest in order to close the incision. It wasn't until much later, after I had regained some strength, that I learned I'd nearly died from the infection.

By this time, I'd had several close encounters with death. I don't remember those days very well, but I do know that I was prepared to die. When you're heading for major surgery or facing a life-threatening situation, you can't avoid wondering if your time is up. That's when you decide whether you're right with God or not. Whether you are ready to step into eternity. I knew I was because I had committed my life to Jesus Christ. While my hope for a healthy existence wavered, my hope in God and his gift of eternal life remained steady.

Life does not stand still for any of us. It is full of changes, large and small. Certainly death is the ultimate and final change; each of us will face it at some time. I'd always thought I was ready, that my faith was strong, but you never really know until you're faced with the immediate prospect of your own death. And in my case there was much more to endure, a greater challenge than I could ever imagine, when I underwent a heart transplant—and survived.

For me, whatever the wind blows my way, hope is constant. I love to sail. When you're out on the water, the wind blows a lot of unsettling conditions your way. So does life. And those unsettling conditions—those changes in our circumstances—can break us or make us. It's not how we handle the good days that determines how well we do in life. It's how we handle the bad days.

It is hope in God that lights my way along life's path and shines a comforting glow on death's door. That is why I always trust in the Lord and hope for the best.

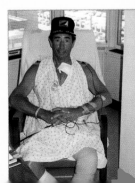

Rich DeVos recovers after his initial bypass surgery in 1983, the first in a series of serious health challenges.

Lesson

PERSI

2

STENCE

You'll never know what you might accomplish

until you try. That truth is so simple that some

people completely overlook it.

RICH DEVOS

Early in life, Rich DeVos
learned important lessons
in persistence.

PERSISTENCE

W hen our children were small, Helen and I would often read to them. One of their favorite books—and mine—was the classic, *The Little Engine That Could.* This simple story of the little engine that made it up the highest hills, puffing, "I think I can, I think I can," has thrilled the hearts of millions of children for more than two generations. With its simple vocabulary and illustrations that seem wonderfully naïve by today's standards, this book has managed to convey a truth that is equally applicable to both children and adults: *If you persist, you will succeed.* "I think I can, I think I can," will become, "I thought I could, I thought I could."

Persistence is the single most important ingredient of success in life. It involves determination and the will to persevere, no matter what the obstacle. If you are willing to stumble and fall and still keep on going, then you will succeed. If you get knocked down a hundred times, yet jump up and say, "Here goes 101!" then you will succeed. Like that little locomotive that repeated "I think I can," you *will* succeed.

But be careful. There is a difference between persistence and stubbornness. Don't confuse determination with mule-headedness. They're not the same. Stubbornness leads to the dead ends of

foolish and unproductive behavior; persistence moves you forward. Stubbornness disconnects you from reality and can result in paralyzing inaction. Persistence keeps you connected to life and helps you maintain momentum.

Persistence has a purpose. It flows from a decision and toward a goal. Stubbornness is random and aimless. It annoys people. If you are willing to buck the odds and persist in your goals, people will often get behind you and push, but if you are just plain obstinate, then people will simply move around you and go on. It's your choice.

Much of what I learned about persistence I learned early in life from my grandfather. He was an old-fashioned "huckster," a term, appropriately enough, that comes from an old Dutch word that means "to peddle." My granddad drove to the farmer's market every day in his old truck and bought vegetables, which he then sold door-to-door to the people in our neighborhood. Whatever was left over at the end of the day, I would sell. My grandfather was with me the first time I sold something—a batch of onions left over after he had finished his regular route. Under his watchful eye, I made my first sale, a transaction that netted only a few pennies but taught me a lesson in persistence that would pay dividends for a lifetime. After that, whenever my grandfather had vegetables left over, I sold them. It took persistence, but I loved it.

Rich DeVos' ancestors strongly influenced his life through their faith and values.

Early in my high school days, I had another experience that taught me the value of making tough decisions and persisting in following through on those decisions. When I was a fifteen-year-old freshman, my parents sent me to a small Christian high school in our city. Like most teenagers, I didn't think about the fact that private schools cost money or that my parents had to sacrifice to pay my tuition. I just chased the girls and goofed off and didn't pay much attention to grades. Somehow I managed not to flunk anything that first year, but I passed Latin solely because I promised never to take the class again!

> *Little decisions accumulate and pile up until they amount to a big one that seems inevitable. The sum total of many small decisions is one big decision.*

At the end of the academic year, my father said, "If you're just going to fool around, then I'm not going to pay all that extra money to keep you in a private school." So my sophomore year I went to the public high school. By the end of that year, however, I knew that I wanted to be back with my friends at the Christian school. When I told my father, he said, "If you want it, you'll have to pay for it yourself."

The decision was mine—and so was the responsibility. If I chose the Christian high school, I would have to pay the freight. And that would take real persistence. After some serious thought, I chose to return to the Christian school and decided I could pay the bill myself.

That was the first time in my life that I'd consciously made a decision of any magnitude, but it felt good to have a goal, to work toward something I really wanted. I had a part-time job at a gas station and thought I could earn enough money to pay the tuition—but barely. I filled tanks, washed windshields, saved my money, and made tuition payments. And guess what? After I demonstrated some real determination, my parents stepped in to help. If I was willing to persist, then they were willing to pay.

It's amazing how much of our lives are shaped by small decisions. My decision to go back to a Christian school and pay my own way wasn't a huge decision—at least in the greater scheme of things—but it had a profound effect on my life. Little decisions accumulate and pile up until they amount to a big one that seems inevitable. The sum total of many small decisions is one big decision.

So once you set a goal and decide to pursue it with all your heart, then the next step is to calculate the cost.

I recall the time when my partner, Jay, and I considered buying our first company jet. First, the plane manufacturer offered to give us a ride. That was easy to say "yes" to. Next, they offered to leave the plane in town for a couple weeks for us to use. And that was easy to say "yes" to. Then they tried to take the airplane back! This time we said "no!" and bought it. A series of small decisions had led to one very big one.

Whether large or small, making decisions means setting goals for yourself. And it takes real courage to do that. Especially when it is a

Prior to co-founding Amway, Rich DeVos and his friend Jay Van Andel started a drive-in restaurant business, each taking turns cooking and waiting on customers.

major decision. Because if you dare to grab destiny by the throat and make a tough, important decision, it will change your life.

But decisions that inflict no pain, or require no commitment, or are pursued without passion or persistence, seldom result in a real reward. So once you set a goal and decide to pursue it with all your heart, then the next step is to calculate the cost. If you know in advance that the pursuit of your goal will require both time and commitment, then you will not be deterred later.

Jay and I started one of the largest direct-sales companies in the world. And over the years, I have spoken to hundreds of thousands of people about starting a second career with Amway. But I have never tried to make it sound easy. It isn't easy. It wasn't easy for us. When people came to us with the expectation of quick prosperity, I told them to look elsewhere.

There are few, if any, shortcuts to success. But there is something uniquely satisfying about earning your success through hard work. And when you set a goal and make the commitment to work for it, even when you're tired or discouraged, it is persistence that will carry you through.

If you're an aspiring entrepreneur with no money and a big dream, then you've probably heard people say, "Are you crazy?" I certainly did. People may think you're persistently nuts rather than tenaciously diligent

> *When confronted with a failure or a disappointment, you have only two choices: You can give up, or you can persist.*

in the pursuit of your goal. If I had listened to some of my friends and many of my critics, I would never have gone into business on my own. But Jay and I were "crazy" enough to follow our dream and persist . . . and that dream became a multibillion-dollar company!

Many big dreams begin with vague ideas. When I started out, my goal was simple: I wanted to be in business for myself. I was prepared to make sacrifices (consistent with my values) to achieve that aim, but I didn't really know where it would lead or how I would do it. In the beginning Jay and I made it from milestone to milestone, seldom able to look very far ahead. We just persisted. When our fledgling company made its first million dollars in sales, we began thinking about the second. When we outgrew our first building, we constructed another. Gradually, through consistent, persistent effort, we built a large, successful global company.

If we had looked for reasons to be discouraged, we could have found them. The pathway of life is full of would-be roadblocks and distractions. For example, early in our careers, we planned a big sales meeting and promoted it through radio and newspaper ads. We canvassed people and rented an auditorium for the event. Despite our effort, however, it was a disaster! Only two people showed up. It's tough to make a powerhouse sales speech to an empty auditorium. After it was over, we drove home in the middle of the night because we didn't have any money for a motel room. But that setback didn't stop us. When confronted with a failure or a disappointment, you have only two choices: You can give up, or you can persist.

If I could pass on one character trait to young people in the world—one single quality that would help them achieve success in life—it would be persistence. It's more important than intellect, athletic ability, good looks, or personal magnetism. Persistence comes from a deep place in the soul. It is a God-given compensation for what we lack in other areas of our life. Never underestimate its power.

Under the watchful eye of his grandfather—Peter Dekker, a vegetable peddler—Rich DeVos made his first sale, a transaction that netted only a few pennies, but provided a lifelong lesson in persistence.

Lesson
3
C O N F I

More than any other single lesson,

my experiences have conspired to teach me

the value of determined, confident effort.

RICH DEVOS

Rich DeVos' and Jay Van Andel's Caribbean adventure aboard the *Elizabeth* was cut short when they sank off the coast of Cuba. The men learned lessons for a lifetime in confidence and risk-taking.

CONFIDENCE

O ne of life's great ironies is the fact that people who shoot low are often great shots. They aim for nothing and usually hit it. But the most powerful forces in the world can be those who dare to aim high and keep on practicing, day after day, until they hit their target. And what fuels that kind of persistence? Confidence. If you don't believe in your potential to reach a goal, then you probably won't keep on trying. But like "the little engine that could," if you say to yourself "I think I can," you probably will.

What ultimately motivates people is often a mystery to me. Yet I've been described as a great motivator, and I am frequently asked to make motivational speeches. People want me to tell them what makes some people succeed and others fail. They want to know "the secret to success."

I wish I had some profound wisdom to share. I wish I could explain why some people move forward when others quit. But I am certain of one thing: Almost everyone can do whatever they set out to do if they have confidence that they can. And that's a choice. We choose to be confident. We choose to believe in ourselves and in our goals.

When I was a young man deciding what to aim for in life, I wasn't particularly interested in getting a Ph.D., or in entering politics, or in becoming a PGA golfer. All of those things are admirable goals, but they didn't appeal to me. What I wanted—my goal—was to build and succeed in my own business. And I never had any doubt that I could do exactly that.

You could argue that my confidence was a gift from God or a genetic endowment of some sort. I do believe that every good gift comes from God, and it's certainly possible that I may have inherited an entrepreneurial gene or two. The important point, however, is that *anyone* can choose to have such confidence. Confidence is both a choice and a gift. If you didn't receive the gift, then you can make the choice. And when you make the choice, you receive the gift. It's like the old chicken and egg question; it really doesn't matter which comes first.

As I look back over my seventy-plus years, I can see clearly that confidence has been a fundamental and defining personal trait of my life.

> *Confidence is both a choice and a gift. If you didn't receive the gift, then you can make the choice. And when you make the choice, you receive the gift.*

When I was young man, I had a brash and sometimes unjustified sense of confidence. But I'm glad I did. Failure and risk-taking often go hand in glove. If you're not willing to risk failure, then you're not likely to take many risks. I believed that I had the potential to do anything, and as a result, I did things that no cautious or "reasonable" person would attempt. In the process, I had fun and experienced some incredible adventures; I also learned valuable lessons that have stayed with me for my entire life.

One of those lessons came when I was in my early twenties. Still single and footloose, my best friend, Jay Van Andel, and I decided to buy a sailboat and sail to South America. We wanted a year of great adventure, and we set out to get it.

First, we traveled to the Atlantic coast, where we found an old, wooden Nova Scotia schooner, named the *Elizabeth*. It had been languishing in dry dock for years. We didn't know the first thing about buying a boat, and if I'd known then what I know now, we'd have run, not walked, away from that thirty-eight footer.

The name *Elizabeth* means "God is good fortune." As we were to find out, however, the *Elizabeth* was poorly named. In fact, the only thing worse than the condition of that boat was our sailing skills. But we weren't about to let inexperience get in our way.

Our plan was to sail the boat down the East Coast of the United States and then to Cuba (this was the pre-Castro era); from there, we would continue through the Caribbean to South America. This was an ambitious trip, even for experienced sailors, but we had an overabundance of youthful confidence and were ready for the challenge.

When we bought the *Elizabeth*, I had never set foot on the deck of a sailboat. I wasn't even qualified to be called a novice. Instruction book in one hand and tiller in the other, we ran aground all the way down the East Coast of the United States. I can't tell you how many times our log book read "Aground again!"

Not surprisingly, navigation wasn't our strong suit either. At one point, we got so lost in New Jersey that it took the Coast Guard eight hours to find us. Part of the problem was that we weren't even in the ocean. We took two wrong turns on the Intracoastal Waterway and got stuck in some bayou.

Just as we were getting the hang of it, we realized that getting lost and running aground were the least of our problems. We eventually made it to Cuba, but while sailing along the north coast of the island, the boat began to take on water. We put in at a small harbor for repairs and spent two weeks recaulking the hull of the *Elizabeth*. Then we recruited a Cuban seaman to crew for us, and we set sail out into the Bahamas Channel. Unfortunately, the new caulking was worse than the old!

In the middle of the night, in 1,500 feet of water, we started to sink. No amount of pumping could keep up with the leaks. As the bilge and then the cabin slowly filled with water, we prepared to abandon ship. Shooting off our flare gun and blinking "SOS" with our flashlights, we scanned the horizon for any sign of a ship. At 2:30 A.M. the *Adabelle Lykes*, an American freighter, pulled alongside and rescued us. By dawn, the *Elizabeth* was at the bottom of the sea. It was no *Titanic* moment, you understand. She just leaked and went down.

The captain of the *Adabelle Lykes* put us ashore in San Juan, Puerto Rico. At that point,

Upon their return from South America in 1949, Rich DeVos and Jay Van Andel hold the salvaged life ring and share memories to last a lifetime after their ill-fated voyage aboard the *Elizabeth*.

most people would have given up and gone home, but Jay and I were committed to our dream and were still confident that we could make it work. And we weren't afraid of risk or adventure. We had managed to salvage most of our personal possessions and still had a little cash,

so we decided to continue. After all, there were other ways to get around South America.

In Puerto Rico, we signed on as deckhands on an old tramp tanker that was bound for the island of Curaçao in the Dutch Antilles, just off the coast of Venezuela. From there we flew on a prop plane to Caracas, then on to the Colombian highlands, where we tra-

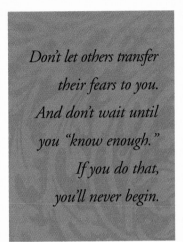

Don't let others transfer their fears to you. And don't wait until you "know enough." If you do that, you'll never begin.

veled on a paddle-wheel steamer up the Magdalena River. We then transferred to a narrow-gauge railroad and headed for the Pacific Coast.

By the time we arrived back home, we had traveled down the entire West Coast of South America, from Colombia to Chile, flown over the Andes, and then traveled up the East Coast all the way to what was then Guiana. We stopped at every place that interested us, and then for good measure, we visited most of the major islands in the Caribbean. It was a wonderful, once-in-a-lifetime adventure.

That trip changed my life. I had learned to take risks and to rise above defeat in order to achieve a goal and realize a dream. The sinking of the *Elizabeth* had only heightened my sense of "living in the moment," and it had taught me to improvise in ways that made life more interesting and spontaneous. Every subsequent venture in my life has benefited from the lessons learned on that trip.

Confidence is often rooted in the irrational hope that things will work out. Don't let your dreams die for lack of confidence. Don't let others transfer their fears to you. And don't wait until you "know enough." If you do that, you'll never begin. You'll never learn everything you need to know until you start doing. You'll never learn to sail by standing on the shore. At some point you have to stop thinking, stop talking, stop weighing the arguments and counting the costs, and simply launch out.

How will you ever know what you can accomplish if you never try? "Try or cry," that's my slogan. Either try or stop crying about it. Confidence will come in the *doing*.

Despite the fact that neither of them knew how to fly, Rich DeVos and his friend, Jay Van Andel, started Wolverine Air Service as one of their early business ventures, proving that confidence and the will to succeed are the key ingredients for any endeavor in life.

Lesson

4

O P T I

If you have that flame

of a dream down inside you somewhere,

thank God for it, and do something about it.

And don't let anyone else blow it out.

RICH DEVOS

Rich DeVos and Jay Van Andel, partners
and Amway co-founders, enjoy a moment
together in 1986 on the occasion of the
company's 25th anniversary.

Portrait by David LaClaire

OPTIMISM

I f you expect something to turn out badly, it probably will. Pessimism is seldom disappointed. But the same principle also works in reverse. If you expect good things to happen, they usually do! There seems to be a natural cause-and-effect relationship between optimism and success.

Optimism and pessimism are both powerful forces, and each of us must choose which we want to shape our outlook and our expectations. There is enough good and bad in everyone's life—ample sorrow and happiness, sufficient joy and pain—to find a rational basis for either optimism or pessimism. We can choose to laugh or cry, bless or curse. It's our decision: From which perspective do we want to view life? Will we look up in hope or down in despair?

I believe in the upward look. I choose to highlight the positive and skip right over the negative. I am an optimist by choice as much as by nature. Sure, I know that sorrow exists. I am in my seventies now, and I've lived through more than one crisis. But when all is said and done, I find that the good in life far outweighs the bad.

An optimistic attitude is not a luxury; it's a necessity. The way you look at life will determine how you feel, how you perform, and how well you will get along with other people. Conversely, negative

> *The way you look at life will determine how you feel, how you perform, and how well you will get along with other people.*

thoughts, attitudes, and expectations feed on themselves; they become a self-fulfilling prophecy. Pessimism creates a dismal place where no one wants to live.

Years ago, I drove into a service station to get some gas. It was a beautiful day, and I was feeling great. As I walked into the station to pay for the gas, the attendant said to me, "How do you feel?" That seemed like an odd question, but I felt fine and told him so. "You don't look well," he replied. This took me completely by surprise. A little less confidently, I told him that I had never felt better. Without hesitation, he continued to tell me how bad I looked and that my skin appeared yellow.

By the time I left the service station, I was feeling a little uneasy. About a block away, I pulled over to the side of the road to look at my face in the mirror. How did I feel? Was I jaundiced? Was everything all right? By the time I got home, I was beginning to feel a little queasy. Did I have a bad liver? Had I picked up some rare disease?

The next time I went into that gas station, feeling fine again, I figured out what had happened. The place had recently been painted a bright, bilious yellow, and the light reflecting off the walls made everyone inside look as though they had hepatitis! I wondered how many other folks had reacted the way I did. I had let one short conversation with a total stranger change my attitude for an entire day. He told me I looked sick, and before long, I was actually feeling sick. That single negative observation had a profound effect on the way I felt and acted.

The only thing more powerful than negativism is a positive affirmation, a word of optimism and hope. One of the things I am most thankful for is the fact that I have grown up in a nation with a grand tradition of optimism. When a whole culture adopts an upward look, incredible things can be accomplished. When the world is seen as a hopeful, positive place, people are empowered to attempt and to achieve.

In the absence of optimism, however, we are left with nothing but critics, naysayers, and prophets of doom. When a nation expects the worst from its people and institutions and its experts focus exclusively on faults, hope dies. Too many people spend too much time looking down rather than up, finding fault with their country's political institutions, economic system, educational establishment, religious organizations, and—worst of all—with each other.

Faultfinding expends so much negative energy that nothing is left over for positive action. It takes courage and strength to solve the genuine problems that afflict every society. Sure, there will always be things that need fixing. But the question is, Do you want to spend your time and energy tearing things down or building them up?

The staging of a Broadway show could illustrate my point. Let's say a new production is about to open. A playwright has polished the script, investors have put up the money, and

When Rich DeVos married Helen, shown here with her parents George and Wilma VanWesep, he was blessed with a family who shared his deep belief in God.

the theater has been rented. A director has been chosen, actors have been auditioned and selected, and the cast has been rehearsing for weeks. Set, lighting, and sound engineers have been hard at work. By the time opening night arrives, nearly a hundred people have labored tirelessly—all working long hours to make magic for their audience.

> *It is much easier to criticize than to create. When we revere the critics of society, we eventually become a society of critics, and when that happens, there is no room left for constructive optimism.*

On opening night, four or five critics sit in the audience. If they pan it, the play will probably close in a matter of days or weeks. If they praise it, the production could go on for a long and successful run. In the end, success or failure might hinge on the opinion of a single person—someone who might be in a bad mood on opening night!

What's wrong with this scene? In one sense, nothing. Critics have a legitimate role. The problem arises when we make critics our heroes or put them in control of our fate. When we empower the critic more than the playwright, something is wrong. It is much easier to criticize than to create. When we revere the critics of society, we eventually become a society of critics, and when that happens, there is no room left for constructive optimism.

We need to honor those who create and take risks. When we discredit problem solvers and creators, innovation is stifled. People instinctively hold back when they know their work will be subjected to the cynicism of a heartless critic. When we encourage negativism too much, when we honor the critics more than the creators, we run the risk of producing a generation that only knows how to tear things down.

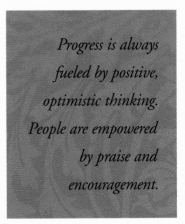

Progress is always fueled by positive, optimistic thinking. People are empowered by praise and encouragement.

In the 1960s, Ralph Nader became a national celebrity by criticizing the automobile industry. In fairness to him, it must be said that the auto industry needed some improving. But it's also important to recognize that Ralph Nader never built an automobile. Today, this industry skillfully mass-produces modern cars and sells them at a price that most people can afford. It is a complex process, but it is accomplished so expertly that few of us appreciate the difficulty of the task. It's far easier to find fault with your car and take it for granted. What impresses me most is not what's wrong with our cars but what's right. What a marvelous accomplishment that finished vehicle represents.

If you think most people are slow-witted or incompetent (as many critics do), or that every big industry is hopelessly corrupt and greedy, then it's unlikely that you will be working hard to make things better. Pessimism, cynicism, the downward look—all of these attitudes lead to paralysis and inaction. If you believe the system can't be fixed, then you'll never make the attempt. Progress is always fueled by positive, optimistic thinking. People are empowered by praise and encouragement.

We live in a marvelous age, yet I know a lot of people who are consumed by nostalgia for the "good old days." They are continually pessimistic about the present and the future. They think that if the economy is good, then social values must be bad. If the national crime rate is down, then private immorality must be up. While I have fond memories and great respect for those who have gone before me, I do not pine for the past. I choose to live in the present and be optimistic about the future. And I have good reason to feel that way!

When our nation was established, the average life expectancy was

When you're an optimist, you're more concerned with problem solving than with useless carping about issues.

less than forty years of age. For men, a typical workweek was seventy-two hours. For women, it was worse. Women worked at home nearly one hundred hours a week, and they did so without the benefit of modern appliances. People seldom traveled more than two hundred miles from their birthplace in their entire lifetime, and most got no further than a day's walk. Disease was commonplace, the infant mortality rate was high, wealth was not widely distributed, and slavery was widespread. Does that sound like "the good old days" to you?

Optimism doesn't need to be naïve. You can be an optimist and still recognize that problems exist and that some of them are not dealt with easily. But what a difference optimism makes in the attitude of the problem solver. For example, through the years I've heard some people say that the money spent on our space program has been wasted. "Instead of spending $455 million dollars to put a man on the moon," they say, "why not spend that money here on earth on the poverty problem?" But when you ask them exactly how they would spend that money to solve the poverty problem, most of them don't have an answer. "Give me a solution," I tell them, "and I'll raise you the money." Think in positive terms about how to address the issue rather than criticizing money spent on another program, such as America's space program, which resulted in many positive discoveries that have benefited mankind.

Optimism diverts our attention away from negativism and channels it into positive, constructive thinking. When you're an optimist, you're more concerned with problem solving than with useless carping about issues. In fact, without optimism, issues as big and on-going as poverty have no hope of solution. It takes a dreamer, someone with hopelessly optimistic ideas, great persistence, and unlimited confidence to tackle a problem that big. It's your choice.

Lesson

5

R E S P

E C T

The man who becomes a great leader

usually has a respect for his followers that is

as deep and real as their respect for him.

RICH DEVOS

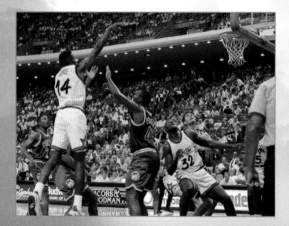

As chairman and owner of the NBA
Orlando Magic, Rich DeVos' leadership
skills apply as well to managing a sports
team as they do to running a business.

RESPECT

A s owner of both the NBA Orlando Magic and the WNBA Orlando Miracle teams, I sometimes hear players say, "I don't get any respect." The center of attention in high school and college, these professionals often do not receive the same notice in the tough competition of the NBA or WNBA. They may not get as much playing time or as much praise from the fans. When that happens, some of them begin to equate this lack of attention with a lack of respect. Other players focus on the attention given to them by the media—points scored per game, turnovers, blocks, and so on—and use it as a measure of how much they are respected.

Unfortunately, some of these players don't understand that respect begins with them. It's driven by their own inner strength, by knowing who they are as creatures of God, by loving and respecting themselves— not by their amount of playing time or by the amount of attention they get from the fans or the media.

Of course, there are also those players who relate respect to how much money they earn in comparison to other players. If another player makes more money, they view that person as receiving more respect. Again, they don't understand that respect begins with how you value yourself as a person, regardless of how much money you get paid.

> *Every person is a human being created in the image of God with a purpose and place in life.*

Some people say that love makes the world go round. But in practical terms, in our day-to-day contact with people, *respect* is what makes the world go round. Every person is a human being created in the image of God with a purpose and place in life. If we operate by this standard, we dignify other human beings by treating them as we ourselves wish to be treated. When we do this, we affirm and empower them in meaningful and concrete ways. We show them respect.

If we do not operate by this standard, we demean and dismiss others according to our own prejudices. If we categorize or stereotype people, we rob them of their dignity. Our standard of measurement must never be the color of someone's skin or their religion, what school they attend, what neighborhood they live in, what kind of car they drive, what clothes they wear, or what language they speak. If we throw up such barriers, if we see people only as labels, then we are not seeing them as human beings with potential and intelligence. Too often we judge people by their vocations, overlooking their competence and their unique and essential gifts.

The "ordinary" folks are the backbone of every nation. They are the men and women who get the job done. They are the unsung, salt-of-the-earth heroes of society. I met just such a man one summer when my family and I were staying at a vacation cottage. This fellow was the garbage collector in that area, and he was the best at his job

I'd ever seen. Once a week this man showed up at precisely 6:30 in the morning. You could set your clock by him. As he moved among the cottages, he didn't throw the trash can noisily in the general direction of the truck and hope it hit the target. With an effortless grace he lifted the can, emptied the garbage into the truck, returned the can to the side of the road, and carefully put the lid back in place. He worked quietly and discreetly, a meticulous man who made a physically demanding job look easy.

After observing this man in action for a couple weeks, one morning I went out to greet him when he arrived. "You're doing a great job," I told him.

"Are you just getting home or just leaving?" he asked. I guess he couldn't imagine that anyone would get out of bed just to pay him a compliment.

"Neither," I said. "I came out to tell you that I really appreciate the good job you're doing."

As I said that, he gave me a big smile. Then he told me that in his twelve years of hauling garbage, no one had ever said a kind word to him, including his boss. For twelve years, that garbage collector had done his job well, with dignity, without ever hearing a word of encouragement or thanks. That man had self-respect.

> The "ordinary" folks are the backbone of every nation. They are the men and women who get the job done. They are the unsung, salt-of-the-earth heroes of society.

Respect begins with how you feel about yourself, not what others say about you. Respect begins with knowing who you are, loving yourself, and accepting yourself.

Everyone is worthy of respect as an individual and as a productive citizen—and I mean everyone. I know there are people with problems and shortcomings. I know there are people who are lazy and unreliable and won't work. But how many people *did* go to work today? In the United States alone, it was over 125,000,000. Most people get up every day and go to work in every walk of life. They are the people who make society *work*. Without them, life would be chaos.

Over the years, I've thought long and hard about what constitutes a good leader and about what particular qualities make a person effective. I've concluded that respect for others is the most essential trait a leader must possess. The nuts and bolts of running a business or an organization are important, but they are of little consequence if you don't respect the people with whom you work—your colleagues, your employees, and your customers. And if they don't respect *you*, then you're not a leader.

Respect is reciprocal; "What goes around comes around." In other words, if you want to be respected, you must respect others. If you don't give it, then you won't get it back. People know when you value and respect them—and they know when you don't. You can't hide disrespect. People understand your attitude instinctively, even when they can't put it into words.

Rich DeVos and Jay Van Andel—friends, partners, and co-founders of Amway—have always maintained a deep sense of respect for one another.

Respect isn't something you demand. It has to be earned. Years ago, I spent a week aboard the *Enterprise,* a motor yacht we used to host gatherings for high-achieving Amway distributors.

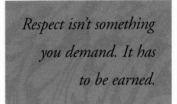

Respect isn't something you demand. It has to be earned.

At the time, we had a new captain, and early in the week, he pulled me aside. He then told me that even though he "demanded respect" from the crew, he wasn't getting it. I told him that respect must be earned; it cannot be demanded. Over the course of the week, it became clear to me that the captain didn't share that view. He "demanded" respect, and he did not show respect to others—in this case, his crew. He wasn't with us very long.

I am frequently asked to speak to different groups, and lately I've been opening my talks with the simple affirmation, "I'm a sinner, saved by grace." In a society obsessed with social status and wealth, it's important to recognize that we *all* fall short of meeting God's standards. None of us can respect another person if we think we're morally superior. But remember this: Jesus saved his harshest criticism for religious hypocrites—for those people who respected no one but themselves.

Think of all the people with whom you come into regular contact—family, friends, customers, clients, and colleagues. They all touch your life in some unique or special way. How many of those people know that you respect them for what they do and who they are? You may admire and need them, but have you said so? Tell them. Show them. Give them the respect they deserve. Make your respect for them tangible. It's what makes the world go round.

One of the most powerful

forces in the world is

the will of men and women

who believe in themselves,

who dare to hope and aim high,

who go confidently after the things

they want from life.

RICH DeVos

Lesson

ACCOUN

6

Everyone is accountable to someone.

RICH DEVOS

Rich DeVos credits his wife, Helen, with being
a beacon of faith for him and their children.

ACCOUNTABILITY

ccountability is as old as the Garden of Eden. When Adam and Eve took a bite of that apple, they both tried to "pass the buck." Adam blamed Eve, and Eve blamed the serpent. But before the day was over, both were held accountable for their actions.

When we read these excuses, it's tempting to laugh. When Adam and Eve got caught, their responses were pitiful: "She made me do it" . . . "It's all the snake's fault." But we shouldn't laugh too hard because we can easily lapse into the same kind of blaming. God gave us free will. We can make choices—but we must take responsibility for those choices.

Everyone is accountable to someone. Accountability is the glue that holds society together. It is the social contract that dictates how we should act in relation to each other. At least that's the theory. In practice, this social contract is both tangible and intangible. The tangible contract is our country's laws. The intangible, but more important, contract is reflected in our own personal values, which is our accountability. It arises in our day-to-day lives from an individual belief in certain principles. It is an inner commitment to outward behavior.

The notion that each of us is responsible for what we do—and that good behavior should be rewarded and bad behavior punished—is so fundamental that it was never seriously challenged until the middle of

Even in the worst of situations, on the most uneven playing field, countless people make good decisions, hold themselves accountable, and achieve their goals.

the twentieth century. Unfortunately, in many circles today, the notion of personal responsibility has lost its luster. Some cultural critics would lead us to believe that no one is really accountable for their actions, that people are solely the product of social forces.

In response to these critics, I can admit that many people face huge obstacles to responsible behavior. The playing field isn't always level, and those in dire circumstances may face great temptations and even greater obstacles. There is also no doubt that some people have to climb higher than others to achieve success in life. However, if we claim that some folks are not responsible for their actions because of the poor environment in which they live, then we have to assume that they really don't have freedom of choice. And that's just not true. Every human being has a choice.

To claim that some people do not have a choice, that they do not have free will, can take away their responsibility for their actions. It reduces them to little robots, programmed by society, and it dishonors all those who *have* succeeded while living in the same conditions. Even in the worst of situations, on the most uneven playing field, countless people make good decisions, hold themselves accountable, and achieve their goals.

The idea that people are puppets and social conditions are the strings is a terrible kind of bigotry. It implies that some folks are endowed with the wisdom and power to control their own lives and others are merely jerked along by society, that they are either too weak or ignorant to make intelligent choices.

This kind of "scapegoating" has become a national pastime. Our scapegoats are the school system, the criminal justice system, big government, and big business. Unfortunately, we've come a long way from the ancient Jewish tradition from which we've borrowed the word *scapegoat*. In fact, we've turned the whole idea on its head.

For the ancient Jews, the Day of Atonement was a time when the people were cleansed of their sins. It was a time of communal self-reflection and repentance, and no one was exempt—from the king to the lowliest shepherd boy, everyone participated. Even the great high priest, before he could carry out his official duties, had to confess his own sins and the sins of his household. Then, in a dramatic public ceremony, the high priest would tie a scarlet cord around the neck of a goat—the scape-goat—which represented the sins of the people. He then would send the animal out of the city gates, and it would symbolically carry the sins of the people into the wilderness.

The scapegoat was a symbol of personal accountability; it was not a convenient device to blame someone else. The ancient tradition was a confession of personal and national failure and an admission of responsibility.

I'm not suggesting that we go back to this ritual, but I am suggesting that the underlying principles of the Day of Atonement still apply. The tradition of the scapegoat was all about confessing and being forgiven. Everyone is accountable for what they do, both individually and collectively. Only when we take full responsibility for our actions can we shed the burdens of our mistakes and go forward.

> *Only when we take full responsibility for our actions can we shed the burdens of our mistakes and go forward.*

In recent years, I have seen this kind of accountability firsthand in the world of sports. I have known many star basketball players who have overcome great obstacles and gone on to fame and fortune. Many of the players on the Orlando Magic and Miracle teams have come from one-parent homes where their mothers inspired them to do their best. One of our players could not play basketball unless he got all As in school. His mother held him accountable because she knew he was capable of achieving high grades. He got all As and received a scholarship to a Big Ten school. He graduated and now plays in the NBA.

Accountability is always about *assuming* responsibility, not deferring it. Unfortunately, we live in a time when our national leaders seldom admit sin—even when caught red-handed—and when people at every level of public life avoid accountability. Rather than "'fess up," we cover up. Instead of telling the whole truth, we engage in "spin control," a euphemism for putting a bad situation in a good light.

Avoiding responsibility has become a full-time job for the spin doctors.

As I have reflected on the issue of accountability over the years, both during my active business life and after my retirement, three principles stand out in my mind. First, the more you have, the greater your accountability. Second, there is no accountability without freedom. Third, there is no accountability without assessment.

> *Unfortunately, we live in a time when our national leaders seldom admit sin— even when caught red-handed—and when people at every level of public life avoid accountability.*

First: The more you have, the greater your accountability. This is illustrated by the biblical parable of the talents which, like the scapegoat, has become such a part of our cultural language that we've forgotten its original, literal meaning. To us a "talent" is any special ability that an individual has, but in Jesus' day the word "talent" referred to a unit of money (Matt. 25:14–30). This becomes particularly relevant when we read Jesus' admonition in another parable: "From everyone who has been given much, much will be demanded" (Luke 12:48). These are words we must take seriously. A person of wealth is "required," in the words of Jesus, to be accountable for the use of that wealth. So if your goal is the accumulation of wealth, then you must be prepared to assume the responsibility that comes with it.

Make no mistake: Whatever our assets might be—financial, personal, position, opportunity, or ability—we are all called to be good stewards of those assets. For that reason, people with public influence have a greater responsibility to set a good example because their lives are so highly visible. Further, people with great intelligence are obligated to use their minds for the public good, and those with artistic genius have a special responsibility to inspire, inform, and instruct. Each of us, in fact, is called to exercise our own particular gifts in pursuit of noble goals. And I firmly believe every person is gifted in some way. The parable of the talents applies to everyone.

Second: There is no accountability without freedom. Accountability and freedom are two sides of the same coin; you can't have one without the other. When I was president of Amway, I quickly learned that it was useless to hold a manager responsible for a certain level of production if I didn't give him the authority to get the job done. If he weren't free to make the decisions, then I couldn't blame him for the results. If we are going to hold people accountable, then we have to create an environment, a society, in which they have the freedom to take risks and make mistakes. We need the freedom to fail and the freedom to advance as far as we can.

> *If we are going to hold people accountable, then we have to create an environment, a society, in which they have the freedom to take risks and make mistakes.*

Before the collapse of communism, marked particularly by the fall of the Berlin Wall and the collapse of the Soviet Union, communist countries, with their bloated bureau-

Rich DeVos' practice of "compassionate capitalism" has become an example throughout the world for many to follow.

Portrait by David LaClaire

cracies, seemed to pride themselves on a lack of accountability. The unbearable pressures of competition, they claimed, would be overcome by an "egalitarian" society in which everyone's job security was guaranteed by the state. In the end, however, the government's guarantee wasn't worth much. An economic system in which no one was given the responsibility of ensuring that a company made money, or that an agency was run efficiently and honestly, was already doomed to failure. Without the freedom to compete—without the freedom to choose, whether that choice ended in success or failure—the communist state resulted in moral and fiscal bankruptcy.

Third: There is no accountability without assessment. It's hard to be accountable without some kind of objective evaluation. We all need help in assessing our personal performance. For all of my working life I was privileged—in fact, I would say I was blessed—to have a business partner like Jay, who loved me and told me the truth. I always valued his assessment of my business decisions. Without that assessment, I would have made more mistakes. And I did the same for him. We depended on each other because we knew that no one is objective in terms of his own performance.

Evaluation can take many forms. In school, teachers review their students' grades, tests, and performance to assess the students' progress. Because of the human factor, these assessments may not always be impartial, but without tools of evaluation, students would be left in a hopeless mire of mediocrity. A fair system of evaluation nurtures the incentive to work hard and reap the reward. Without regular assessment, hard-working students and teachers—or anyone in any occupation—could not rise above those who don't want to work and are just along for the ride.

We never do anyone a favor by shielding them from the pressures of accountability. Evaluation, whether it is voluntary or mandatory, plays a key role in encouraging excellence. When Jay and I started Amway, evaluations were done every six months. Employees were evaluated not only for pay increases, but also to assess their own goals and hopes.

Of course, it's not a sin to fail. Sometimes evaluations help us find our real gift or ability. If we flounder at one thing, we may find that we need to try something else. James Whistler, the American painter, once recalled how he had flunked a chemistry exam at West Point. "If silicon had been a gas," he said, "I would have been a major general." If he hadn't been subject to that evaluation, we might have had a mediocre soldier instead of a great painter.

Everyone is accountable to someone. Use that accountability to propel you to where you want to go.

Rich DeVos and Jay Van Andel started Amway in 1959 in the basements of their homes and in 1960 purchased a service station in Ada, Michigan, as their new headquarters.

Today Amway is a multibillion-dollar international business. Its headquarters in Ada, Michigan, span well over a mile.

Strong families are made by strong people

who believe enough in the value of their parenthood

that they are willing to arrange their entire lives,

if necessary, around home and family.

RICH DEVOS

Rich DeVos enjoyed a strong sense of family
with his parents, Ethel and Simon, and sisters,
Bernie and Jan.

FAMILY

I have warm memories of my family life, going back to my earliest childhood. We were a close family. We struggled financially sometimes, but we struggled together. There was always plenty of love to go around. My extended family played a key role in teaching me the meaning of love, and my immediate family passed down the Christian values that have been the core of my life. There was never a moment when I felt unloved or alone in facing life's problems.

I can also look back and see clearly how important my family was to my development as a person. My later success in business was built in part on my interest in salesmanship. Much of what I learned early in life about selling, I learned from my grandfather. And I credit my father with instilling in me an entrepreneurial spirit. He was an electrician—a wonderful, hard-working man, as honest as anyone who ever lived. But he was frustrated all his life by the fact that he never owned his own business, and his constant advice to me was one of the most motivating influences in my life. "Whatever you do," he would say, "get in business for yourself." My father died too young—he was only fifty-nine—but he lived long enough to see me achieve a measure of success. And before he died, he reminded me, "Never forget that your business has been built on a foundation of honesty and fairness to others." His admonition has stayed with me all my life.

The home is where love and responsibility are learned and where values are transmitted from one generation to the next. My attitude toward God began as our family bowed our heads around the dinner table, giving thanks for His gifts to us. Today, we often hear the phrase, "The good life." But what is the good life? Is it freedom from oppression and fear? Is it democratic capitalism? Is it financial independence? Is it physical comfort? Is it leisure time? All of these things may be part of "the good life" at any given time, but none of them mean much in the absence of a solid, loving family. The bedrock of democracy, the foundation on which the good life is built, is the institution of the family.

If I were to rank all of the institutions that constitute an ideal society in order of importance, I would have to put family right at the top. Every institution, whether it be representative government, a free-market economy, good schools and universities, or churches and synagogues, depends upon the health of the family for its very survival. The home is so fundamental to human existence that I cannot conceive of any amount of social change or political upheaval that could possibly make it obsolete. Yet, our increasingly complex and fragmented world has put the family under great stress. If we, as individuals and as a society, do not reaffirm our obligation to our spouses and our children, we will pay a terrible price.

> *The bedrock of democracy, the foundation on which the good life is built, is the institution of the family.*

The healthy family depends on a common commitment among the members. The family members make a commitment to each other and to certain values, particularly religious faith. Complacency about such commitment and values can have profoundly negative consequences, and we see those consequences every day in our society—negligent or abusive parents, broken marriages and broken homes, and drug-or alcohol-addicted, underachieving, morally illiterate, or violent children. Without a foundation of spiritual values, our children have no resources to make it through difficult times.

Over the years, like most parents, Helen and I have made mistakes and hit a few bumps in the road. But we've always loved our children fiercely, and when it came time to pass down our values, we did so with diligence and care. We knew that if we were complacent about teaching our children the values of the Christian faith that we hold dear, someone else would do the job. And we might not like the values someone else taught them.

We also avoided "passive parenting"—the notion that says, "It's what you do that counts, not what you say." It's the false belief that somehow your children will learn good values from watching you, even if you never talk about them. Yes, it does matter what you do; if you don't practice what you preach, then you're a hypocrite. But example is not enough. Children need to know *why* parents do what they do. They need parents who actively communicate with them despite their other daily pressures.

There's an old adage that says, "If you're too busy to

Rich DeVos' grandparents passed along a rich heritage of strong faith in God and a deep belief in hard work.

spend time with your family, you're too busy." It's true. Some tasks in life cannot be delegated, and parenthood is one of them. There is no substitute for quality time spent with your family, time when you are genuinely accessible, open to your children, eager to do some of the things *they* want to do. One of the best fathers I've ever known was a man who used to be our company's chief pilot. He was gone a great deal of the time, but when he came home, he was *really* home. He didn't sit around and watch television or hide in the den or spend the weekend on the golf course. When he was home, he made himself accessible to his children, paid attention to them, and spent time with them.

When our children were young, Helen and I taught them values by passing on those broad generalities we call principles, such as honesty and fairness and self-discipline, and also by confronting them with the implications of their specific, day-to-day behavior. Children don't always connect theory and practice, so it's important to make the connection for them.

Today, all of our children are involved in our businesses in one way or another, but none of them stepped into an executive position as though it were their birthright. One of the greatest challenges of running a family-owned business is how to pass it on to the next generation. Fundamental values are often lost from one generation to the next. Jay and I did not want that to happen, so we required all of our children to pay their dues by serving an apprenticeship in the company.

Ever thankful for God's faithfulness through the generations, Rich DeVos enjoys a moment with his grandson, Rick, on his first birthday.

For example, our oldest son, Dick, who eventually succeeded me as president of Amway, went to work at the company when he was twelve years old during his summer vacation. He earned thirty-five cents an hour for pulling weeds and helping to maintain the grounds. Then, over the years, he worked at many other jobs in various departments; he's proud to say that at one point he even got to drive an eighteen-wheeler.

Our other children—Dan, Cheri, and Doug—also were expected to work part-time for the business when they reached an appropriate age. They all held entry-level jobs, and, in the early years, were as anonymous as possible. We wanted them to be judged on the basis of their merits, not their name.

Through their apprenticeships, our children learned to appreciate the real value of all the people who worked long, hard days to make our business a success. They shared their fellow employees' burdens and joys,

> *There is no substitute for quality time spent with your family, time when you are genuinely accessible, open to your children, eager to do some of the things they want to do.*

swapped stories and told jokes, listened and learned. This apprenticeship was not only a way to learn the nuts-and-bolts operation of the company; it was also an opportunity to pass on our values to them.

The line between family values and business values is thin, and businesses need to place an emphasis on the family. For that reason, Jay and I, from the very beginning, did everything we could to promote

> *The line between family values and business values is thin, and businesses need to place an emphasis on the family.*

the health of the families of Amway employees, including the families of distributor business owners, who were the heart of our organization. And this is still true of the company today.

The direct-selling business allows husbands and wives—and even children—to work together. But Jay and I didn't sit down one day and decide, "This is going to be a family-oriented business." It came about naturally because it grew out of our own family values and the Christian concepts that were already an important part of our lives. Gradually, the family emphasis became a key characteristic of our company culture. After a while, we developed specific policies and traditions that encouraged family participation.

I don't pretend to know all the answers to the many questions every parent encounters in child rearing. Sometimes you can fall back on time-tested principles, and sometimes you just have to improvise. Occasionally you put your foot down, and once in a while, it's best to leave well enough alone. You have to know when to be tough and when to be spontaneous, when to cry together and when to laugh. You do your best and trust God for the rest, ever thankful for the most important institution of all: family.

While Rich DeVos' father died an untimely death at age 59, his mother, Ethel, is still living and very much a part of his family.

The DeVos family spent many special times together sailing aboard *Windquest*.

Lesson

FREED

8

I believe in life with a large "YES" and a small "no."

And I believe in affirming every day,

proudly and enthusiastically, that life in America—

under God—is a positive experience.

RICH DEVOS

Rich DeVos credits the military with instilling in him the responsibility and discipline that prepared him for life.

F R E E D O M

O ne day a man decided to sell his house and buy a better one. He called a realtor and asked her to take the listing. The realtor drafted an ad describing the features of the house and placed it in the local paper. The next day the man read the ad—and read it again. Then he went to the telephone and called the realtor.

"I want to cancel the listing," he told her.

"Why?" asked the women in surprise.

"Because I just realized that I *already* live in the house I've always wanted!"

We take a lot of things for granted, don't we? And one of the biggest things most of us take for granted is our democracy—our country and our freedom. Most people appreciate capitalism and the higher living standard it has produced, but far too many folks have no interest in flag-waving or old-fashioned, hand-on-heart patriotism anymore. They think they're too sophisticated. Or they've become complacent. They've forgotten the generations of men and women who fought and died for freedom, who suffered under the Great Depression, and who endured the long, tense standoff between the United States and the Soviet Union.

This complacency has brought pessimism and cynicism. We hear the voices of social critics decrying poverty, crime, alcoholism, divorce,

> *Most people appreciate capitalism and the higher living standard it has produced, but far too many folks have no interest in flag-waving or old-fashioned, hand-on-heart patriotism anymore.*

and abortion ringing in our ears. We also hear pundits spreading cynicism about the political process. Sure, we have problems to solve. But should we define ourselves by our shortcomings or by our strengths?

Fortunately, Americans have a tender national conscience. We have always been alert to the injustices and inequalities that inevitably arise in any human institution. This national conscience has contributed to the elimination of many immoral and unjust practices. Our nation isn't perfect—no human institution is—but the voice of conscience almost always prevails.

At times, however, our national conscience becomes a little too sensitive and our insecurities rise to the surface. Years ago, as communist and socialist governments came into power, many Americans began to ask questions about the free market system and the democratic institutions that sustained it. Was our system really just? Was it working for everyone? A few said "no" and advocated some form of socialist utopia. Others were less motivated by idealism than by revolution. The radical left confused our national insecurity with opportunity. They wanted raw power and a bloody revolution.

Rich DeVos greets a local Boy Scout troop at the community homecoming that celebrated his return from London, where he underwent a successful heart transplant.

In 1959, in the same week that Jay and I founded Amway, Fidel Castro took power in Cuba. While Castro ended the corrupt Batista regime, the country's leadership simply shifted from a right-wing dictator to a left-wing strongman. As Castro's revolution spread to South America, a wave of pessimism swept over many Americans. People said to me, "Capitalism has failed. It is failing around the world." The unfair criticism reminded me of what G. K. Chesterton once said about Christianity: "The Christian ideal has not been tried and found wanting; it has been found difficult and left untried." And so it was with capitalism.

For awhile, the Soviet Union and Cuba were the darlings not only of radicals, but also of some labor unionists and a small but prominent faction of American intellectuals. To my dismay, even some church leaders began to praise communism. In their haste to find fault with capitalism, these defenders excused, denied, or overlooked communism's excesses, abuses, and contradictions. This never made any sense to me. What I didn't understand, to paraphrase Jesus, was why they were picking at the sawdust in the eye of capitalism and overlooking the two-by-four in the eye of communism.

In the 1960s a few old-money aristocrats (who lived in mansions they had inherited and who sheltered their children in fancy private schools) threw parties for young capitalist-bashing radicals (who had trust funds and ivy-league degrees). Somehow, the silliness of it all never occurred to them. The capitalist system they condemned paid their bills and made their lifestyles possible. They were a living contradiction.

A tidal wave of discontent swept over the young people of America. The baby boomers, who were entering high schools and colleges across the nation, began to question the values of their parents. The Vietnam War, the civil rights movement, the environmental movement, the feminist movement, and many other causes kept our nation in constant turmoil. Some people were asking honest questions, wrestling with their consciences. Others exploited the situation for their own gain. But the whipping boy for much of that debate was the very system that made the debate possible.

One day during that time, I was a guest on Larry King's radio show, and one of the callers said to me, "What's the difference between capitalism and communism? In one you're a slave to a state, and in the other you're a slave to the capitalist pigs. Either way you're a slave to somebody." Disillusioned, discouraged, and disheartened, that man was typical of the discontent that had swept over the nation. Caught up in the turmoil of the time, he had no sense of history or any long-term perspective. He had forgotten the incredible accomplishments of the generations that had preceded him. He felt excluded and powerless. But I could not dismiss his feelings of frustration. He'd been hammered by both sides of the debate. He couldn't identify with the self-assured propaganda of the communists, but he also couldn't feel good about a capitalist system that seemed unsympathetic to his dreams. It was a tension felt by many people—and it was very real.

Democratic capitalism had been under attack by the far left, poorly defended by the far right, and taken for granted by most successful capitalists. Ordinary Americans, caught in the middle, didn't know what to believe. They weren't attracted to communism, but they were worried about the future of their nation. In the presence of so much negativism, people lost track of the freedoms they already had.

In response to this, I began making a speech that I called "Selling America." It was my message to the critics of democratic capitalism. Throughout the 1960s, I gave that speech all over the nation. It was my way of reminding people that the winds of freedom and opportunity still blew across America. I was a young man, full of enthusiasm and grateful for the chance to succeed. I wanted to remind everyday Americans that the same system that had empowered the nation to become the world's economic powerhouse, and that gave them the leisure and freedom to be self-critical, also gave them the opportunity to fulfill their dreams.

When I look back on those years in which I was "selling America," I'm amazed at what has happened. My optimism was completely justified. It's hard to find anyone now who is willing to sing the praises of communism, or even socialism for that matter. America has never had it so good. Our economy has grown beyond anyone's most optimistic expectations. The stock market has reached unprecedented levels. More people are employed in our country than ever before. Inflation, which had risen as high as 20 percent in the late 1970s, is down to almost immeasurable levels. New jobs, new businesses, and new industries continue to be created.

Every generation must learn anew to appreciate the rights and privileges that the capitalist system provides.

I am thankful for the economic progress we have made as a nation. I am thankful for the success of my own business enterprises. I am hopeful that nations, particularly those of the former Soviet Union, will eventually find their way and build free economies in which people can realize their dreams.

And I am as optimistic as ever, but I'm cautiously optimistic. Forty years ago, we were insecure and self-questioning. Today, perhaps, we take too much for granted. We are so accustomed to the privileges and opportunities that freedom provides that some of us have come to think of those benefits as entitlements.

Our memories are too short, and many Americans act like spoiled heirs. Rather than working constantly to preserve the opportunities our system provides, they think its benefits are automatic. As a nation we borrow too much, whine too much, and want the government to solve too many problems. Every generation must learn anew to appreciate the rights and privileges that the capitalist system provides. I often think about this when I watch my grandchildren. One of the first phrases children use in fighting over toys is "It's mine!" Possession and private ownership are fundamental instincts. Then, when they get a little older, they say, "Me do!" That simple phrase conveys a confidence in their ability to do even a simple thing like tie a shoelace. And then I hear, "Grandpa, watch me!" They need to be appreciated and applauded for a job well-done.

Capitalism is only as moral or immoral as the people who make it work. Every free person runs the risk of exploiting others, of being greedy, of falling into the trap of consumerism, of avoiding his or her responsibilities to family, nation, and God. But these are the risks we must learn to manage. "Free" enterprise isn't a free gift. We have to work to maintain it.

I think most Americans, if they are candid, feel discomfort when they see the heartrending pictures of starving children in Africa or India or any place in the world where people live in grinding poverty. I would be less than honest if I didn't admit that on occasion, I feel uneasy about the standard of living I enjoy. All of us who reside in comfortable and safe homes, drive air-conditioned cars, and eat three square meals a day must feel a bit uneasy when we are confronted with the reminders of the millions who live in poverty and despair. If we didn't feel that way, something would be desperately wrong, for according to the Bible, we truly are "our brother's keeper."

Those of us who enjoy a high or comfortable standard of living must thank God for what we have and vow daily to be responsible, generous stewards of what we have been given. We must be "compassionate capitalists." I like to remind my children and grandchildren of these words by John Wesley: "Make all you can. Save all you can. Give all you can."

Free people in a free society can choose good, or they can choose evil. They have a choice! The only political or economic system in which we have no risk is one in which we also have no choice. If we forget that, we lose everything.

Rich DeVos' father, Simon, was a hard-working man. He was also a true believer in America and its favorite pastime.

Lesson

Without faith, we are lost,

adrift in the world without an anchor.

RICH DEVOS

Rich DeVos has touched the lives of hundreds of thousands of people with his
remarkable public speaking ability.

F A I T H

As strongly as I believe that hope, persistence, confidence, optimism, respect, accountability, family, and freedom are essential to a successful and rewarding life, I believe even more in the necessity of having a deep, personal faith in God. For me, that means I put my trust in God and in His Son Jesus Christ.

My Christian faith is the foundation on which all else in my life rests; it is my life's most important asset. I believe that genuine success—in every aspect of our lives—depends on an unshakable foundation of Christian faith. Without faith in a personal, creator God, the universe is a meaningless place, nothing in life has direction, and moral principles are impossible. Without faith in the personal God of the Bible, and knowledge of His Word, no one has an accurate road map for life.

Faith is not passive and private. Faith is active. It is something you live and declare. Furthermore, faith gives you something to hang on to in the worst of situations, whether in business or your personal life. When my doctors told me that my heart was failing, I knew that the prognosis was grim and that my options were few. Without my Christian faith, I would have fallen apart and given up. But with Christ strengthening me, I had the will to go on in the face of such overwhelming odds. My faith in God gave me hope.

Uncertainty in the face of powerful, uncontrollable forces is frightening under the best of circumstances. At that moment we are faced with a momentous choice: we can descend into anxiety-ridden confusion, or we can reach out for the vital, living faith in Christ that sustains us and gives us the strength to continue. We can live, or we can die—literally, spiritually, or both.

I believe that genuine success—in every aspect of our lives—depends on an unshakable foundation of Christian faith.

You may be wondering, "If God is real, how do I come to know Him? How do I find that living faith?" That is the good news and the ultimate "hope" that I can share with you. Man is separated from God by sin. But God sent His Son, Jesus Christ, to be born as a child so He could bridge that gap between God and humanity. As a man, Christ died on the cross to pay for our sins. We cannot buy or earn our way to salvation. But the good news is that salvation is a gift from God to all who accept Jesus Christ as their Savior. You can come to know God by admitting that you are a sinner and asking Christ to accept you. All it requires is true faith and a simple prayer. The truth of this is found in the New Testament in the Gospel of John: "For God so loved the world that he gave his one and only Son, that whoever believes in him shall not perish but have eternal life" (John 3:16).

Faith is beyond reason; it fills the gap when you don't know what to do or what's going to happen. It's the choice to go on living, even in the face of death. It's the willingness to take a risk, even when the odds are against you. It's a gift you receive and a choice you make. It's the belief that in the most uncertain and difficult circumstances, whether you can see it or not, there is purpose. In Hebrews, we read, "Faith is the substance of things hoped for, the evidence of things not seen" (11:1, NKJV). It is the knowledge that only one thing is absolutely certain in life—and in death—and that is the love of God.

Faith is a blessing, but sometimes practicing our faith is difficult. For example, it can be hard to believe in a loving God if you do not have loving people around you. Some of the saddest folks I know are those who face uncertainty alone. It is for this reason that God has formed us into units of relationships—from families and friends to the larger community of love, which is His church. In my own life, this begins with family and moves out in expanding circles to include friends from all walks of life.

Faith is beyond reason; it fills the gap when you don't know what to do or what's going to happen. It's the choice to go on living, even in the face of death.

Faith unites families. Over the years, my own family has been close. That's not to say we haven't had problems. Our children are all strong, intelligent people. They have opinions, idiosyncrasies, strengths, and weaknesses. From time to time, we've had issues to work out. We're not afraid to argue, and none of us gives in easily. But when times are tough, we are united. We have a shared list of values, and family loyalty is very high on that list. But at the very top is our faith in God. We stick together not only because we love each other, but because we can look beyond ourselves to Someone much larger than life. Faith gives us perspective.

Sometimes people are surprised to hear a person of wealth or power discuss the importance of spiritual things. But I'm here to tell you that faith matters. Nothing convinces a person of the inadequacy of money or power quite so fast as having some of it! Many people live their whole lives laboring under the illusion that if they only had enough money or power, then all their problems would disappear. Yet if those same people were to acquire a fortune, they would quickly discover just how few problems money can solve! It can't buy you peace of mind. It can't heal broken relationships. It can't give meaning to a life that has none. Money won't soothe a guilty conscience or mend a broken heart. Genuine wealth comes from the hand of God, and real happiness only grows out of faith in Him.

I think it's also important to say, however, that wealth is not necessarily an impediment to faith or spirituality. Material things were put on this earth for people to enjoy. God does not object to that. The Bible tells us not to *worship* material things, not to make idols out of them, but it doesn't tell us not to enjoy the fruits of the earth or of our own labor.

Recognizing the impact of professional sports on the public, Rich DeVos is committed to ensuring that the NBA Orlando Magic exemplifies persistence and hope.

The important thing is that we use the money we have wisely—that we do the best we can with what we've been given. It is when we let money come between us and God that money can corrupt. If we become intoxicated with the power that money brings and forget that the source of our wealth is God, then we become arrogant because we think that we are self-reliant. But we're never really self-reliant. God provides all we have.

> *Genuine wealth comes from the hand of God, and real happiness only grows out of faith in Him.*

Everything we have is truly God's; we only borrow it for a time. No matter what our station in life or what our financial situation might be, God is more interested in the state of our hearts than in the status of our bank accounts. When God blesses us materially, he does so for a reason greater than merely our personal comfort. Those who have money must accept responsibility for that higher purpose. We can never escape the responsibility of God's requirement that we use our wealth in a manner consistent with our faith. Never.

We, as Americans, want to be self-sufficient. In fact, Americans are noted for their notion of "rugged individualism." It is part of our national personality. The likes of John Wayne and Clint Eastwood have been our heroes: the rough, tough man of few words who rides into town and sets things right, then rides off into the sunset, alone. It's a powerful image. We want to have power over our own destiny. We don't want the government to make choices for us, and we don't like folks "messing around" with our lives. We are a "can do" people, full of capable, self-motivated, self-made men and women. The "rugged individual" is part of what has made America the most powerful nation on earth.

In matters of faith, however, we are called to be members of a community. A community of individuals to be sure, but a *community* nevertheless. None of us is self-sufficient in our spiritual lives. We

> *None of us is self-sufficient in our spiritual lives. We need God, and we need each other.*

need God, and we need each other. A lot of people go to church because they think God takes roll. For them, the important thing is to make sure their name gets checked off every Sunday on the heavenly roster. But that's not the way it works. Church is not some kind of moral obligation, some habit or tradition that is "the right thing to do." Church is a place where we worship God, share our faith with the community of believers, build each other up, and get empowered to go out into the world and *live out our faith!*

Similarly, some people think of their spiritual life as if they were one person in a telephone booth, talking to God on a private line. They don't want to be bothered by the demands of "organized religion" and don't think they need anyone else. "Oh yeah, I'm spiritual," they say, "I just don't like church." To those folks I say: You cannot grow spiritually in isolation.

Success is empty and unsatisfying without faith. Without God, life has no purpose or direction, and the good life is impossible. As Jesus said, "What good is it for a man to gain the whole world, yet forfeit his soul?" (Mark 8:36).

Lesson 10

From the fullness of his grace

we have all received one blessing after another.

JOHN 1:16

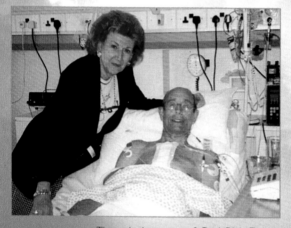

Through the grace of God, Rich DeVos
survived heart transplant surgery. He is
shown here shortly after the surgery
with his wife Helen at Harefield Hospital
in London, England.

G R A C E

hree years ago, I underwent a heart transplant. As I was being wheeled into the operating room, I felt weak and helpless. The risk was high, and the odds of my survival were not very good. Although I didn't welcome death, I knew that I was prepared to meet my God.

It's been said that it's not how a man dies that matters, but how he lives, and I felt that I had lived fully. I'd accomplished most of the goals I had set for myself. I'd lived to see many of my dreams become a reality. I had a strong personal relationship with God. My marriage to a wonderful woman had been long and successful. Our children and grandchildren were healthy and thriving. Physically, I'd led an active, and for the most part, healthy life. I had been blessed with success in business, and to say that God had provided abundantly over the years would be an understatement.

When Drs. Tomatis and McNamara first suggested the possibility of a heart transplant to our oldest son, Dick, they also were totally honest with him about the realities of my situation. In general, there is a shortage of heart donors in the United States, and clinics carefully review every applicant's age, blood and tissue type, lifestyle, and current condition of health. I was nearly seventy, had a rare blood type, and was in poor health.

> *It's been said that it's not how a man dies that matters, but how he lives, and I felt that I had lived fully.*

But the hunt began. The only ones who knew about it were my two doctors and Dick and his wife Betsy—even I was unaware of the search. As my doctors sought out a facility that would even consider accepting me as a heart transplant patient, they gave only my vital statistics. I was a diabetic man in his late sixties with AB positive blood, who had already undergone two bypass operations, barely survived a severe staph infection, and had suffered a stroke. I was a set of statistics—mere probabilities. Not many gamblers would have taken the odds.

The search continued for months, and the results were discouraging. No surgeon or facility in the United States was willing to take my case. Finally, only one possibility emerged. Professor Sir Magdi Yacoub, a thoracic and cardiovascular surgeon at Harefield Hospital in London, agreed to consider my case. Professor Yacoub was known for his leading-edge transplant research. He had performed in the neighborhood of one thousand transplant surgeries and was constantly looking for challenging cases that might provide new or unique circumstances.

Providentially, shortly after Professor Yacoub's name surfaced, Dick was planning to attend a business meeting in Scotland. Without telling anyone else in the family, he made a detour at the conclusion of his Scotland trip and headed for London. Carrying charts, records, test results, and photographs, Dick met with Professor Yacoub. As he had done in the United States, Dick did not talk about who I was in the material sense. He simply presented the medical information.

Professor Yacoub would not say "yes" to a transplant, but he consented to receive progress reports on me. He also indicated that I was fortunate to have the rare blood type that I had. Occasionally, the hospital had an excess of hearts with that particular type, hearts that would otherwise go unused. If it were not for my rare blood type, he said, I wouldn't have *any* chance, not even a remote one, to be considered a transplant candidate.

Dick believed that if Professor Yacoub could meet with me, it might influence his decision in a positive way. When Dick telephoned Professor Yacoub and suggested this, the doctor agreed to a meeting. Now, for the first time, Dick and Betsy, along with Drs. Tomatis and McNamara, told me of the secret they had been carrying for two years. I had considered the idea of a heart transplant, since that seemed to be the only realistic alternative, but I hadn't dwelled on it. Now, my doctors and my family were presenting it to me as a possibility.

> *If it were not for my rare blood type, he said, I wouldn't have any chance, not even a remote one, to be considered a transplant candidate.*

In January of 1997, accompanied by our two younger sons, Dan and Doug, Helen and I flew to London where I endured four days of testing and evaluation. About halfway through the first day, Professor Yacoub asked us all to join him in his office for a private conversation. He had evaluated my medical records and confirmed my condition, but that wasn't enough. It wasn't just science he was concerned about. He wanted to know if I had the will to live. A heart transplant is more than a medical procedure; it is a test of character and will. People who survive must be able to marshal their inner resources and fight to survive. After listening and talking with him for about twenty minutes, I answered his unspoken question by saying, "Yes, I can do this." He paused a moment, then said, "Okay. I will take your case."

> *A heart transplant is more than a medical procedure; it is a test of character and will. People who survive must be able to marshal their inner resources and fight to survive.*

Finding a surgeon willing to accept me as a heart transplant candidate was an amazing accomplishment for my doctors, but it was far from a guarantee that a transplant would ever be done. The second step, of course, was finding a suitable heart—a daunting task when you consider the scarcity of donors and the necessity for a precise blood and tissue match. Complicating the situation even more, the tests revealed that I'd developed a problem with elevated heart pressure. My heart had been straining to overcome chronic edema (the accumulation of fluid in my lungs and other tissues), and the right side had become enlarged to compensate. This meant that a donor heart, in addition to meeting all the other criteria, would also need an enlarged right ventricle. It made the already long odds even longer. Also, since I was a United States citizen, the heart would have to be one that no other citizen in the United Kingdom could use.

Because we had to be within one hour of the hospital at all times, Helen and I moved into a London hotel to wait for a suitable heart to be found. Dick, Dan, Cheri, and Doug and their families took turns visiting us there. I wore a pager, or had it nearby, twenty-four hours a day. No one knew when a heart might become available, but if or when it did, the window of opportunity was short. The longer a donor heart was outside of the host, the less viable it became. The timespan that a heart can be left out of the body is only four hours. All we could do was be available and wait. In the meantime, my health was deteriorating. I was growing weaker every day.

After five months of waiting, almost to the day, the hospital called. A heart had been located, but the circumstances were highly unusual. The hospital had a patient, a thirty-nine-year-old woman who required a lung transplant. In such cases, the surgeons prefer to transplant a new heart and lung as a unit. The lungs function more efficiently with their original heart, and the operation itself is less complex. The hospital had located a heart and lung for the woman from a young man, the victim of an auto accident. Her healthy heart would be surplus. *Precious* surplus.

Professor Yacoub thought the woman's heart would be suitable for me, although he would not know with certainty until the surgical team had removed it. But the truly miraculous link in this chain of events seemed to be that the woman's lung problem had contributed to her developing a larger

than normal right ventricle. Her heart had expanded to compensate for the back-pressure imposed by her impaired lungs. The unusual size of her heart made it unsuitable for anyone else but seemed to make it perfect for me. God certainly is in the details.

I was both thrilled and apprehensive. A patient undergoing open-heart surgery for the first time has a 1 percent mortality rate. Though it is a major surgery, there is a 99 percent chance that the patient will come through alive. With a second or third open-heart surgery, the odds drop to about 50–50. Considering my medical history, I had less than a 50 percent chance of surviving.

I was tired and exhilarated, frightened and hopeful all at the same time. Harefield Hospital was a familiar place by now, but I was flat on my back on a gurney. All I could see was the harsh glare of florescent lights hanging from the ceiling. I could feel the weight of my own body, knowing that I was going to a room where my dying heart would be taken from my chest. If all went well, I'd have a new lease on life, like an old car with a new carburetor. If not, I'd go to a different place—a place I knew about called "heaven," where God is.

Needless to say, I survived. But it was difficult. More difficult than I could ever have imagined. A heart transplant is a harrowing experience, but the aftermath is more difficult than what precedes it: the pain, the drug-induced nightmares, the half-conscious hallucinations, the fear of infection, the fear of my body rejecting the new organ. I had survived, but there was no feeling of euphoria. I couldn't get oriented. For a time, I lost my usual optimism and sense of humor. But ever so slowly, I recovered.

Then, one day, as I was padding down the hall of the hospital, trying to get my aching body working again, I met another patient, a woman. "You've got a new heart?" she asked. It was a pretty easy guess since we were both on the heart transplant ward.

"Yes," I told her.

"When?" she said. "What day, what time, *exactly*, did you get it?"

I told her.

She paused and then smiled. "You have my heart!"

What a miracle! I'd just received a heart transplant and there I was, talking to the donor. She was alive and well and

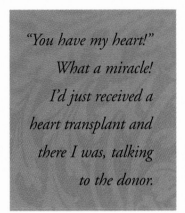

"You have my heart!" What a miracle! I'd just received a heart transplant and there I was, talking to the donor.

recovering from her own miracle. We were *both* alive! Who could have imagined such a possibility?

Three weeks after my transplant, I was released from the hospital. Only the spiritually blind could fail to see the hand of God in my circumstances. But one question remained: Why me? People die every day waiting for a donor organ. I knew that the heart I received would have been thrown out if it hadn't gone to me. There was no one else who could have used it. But I still felt a sense of guilt. I was alive. I had walked out of that hospital with a new heart and a new lease on life, while others still suffered in uncertainty and pain. Ultimately, there was only one explanation for a miracle like that: The grace of God and nothing else.

God's grace gives hope in the most hopeless situations.

EPILO

*The fear of failure keeps us
from trying to succeed.*

*The fear of losing
keeps us from trying to win.*

*The fear of what everyone else will think
keeps us from stepping out boldly.*

*The fear of ridicule
keeps us from declaring our faith in Jesus Christ.*

Most of all, fear stifles hope.

RICH DeVos

A jubilant Rich DeVos enjoys a special home-coming in Grand Rapids, Michigan, with family, friends, and community members following his heart transplant surgery.

EPILOGUE

Even when my transplant operation was over and I was out of the hospital, I was not out of the woods. My body could still reject the heart. Initially, I thought about that every day. I was preoccupied with the fear of rejection. Then, as the weeks passed with no rejection, I began to relax. Three months after the transplant, the doctors said there was a good chance of my heart being accepted by my body.

During that time, one of my grandsons used to pray, "Dear Lord, help Grandpa's other organs to accept his new heart." The Lord answered his and many others' prayers. It has now been three years since I received my new heart, and it is still going strong.

One of the biggest lessons I learned from my transplant experience had to do with that fear of rejection. And I'm often reminded of this lesson because rejection is still a factor in my life. I take anti-rejection medicine every day. And as I think about this, I have come to realize how fear keeps people from doing so many things.

The fear of failure keeps us from trying to succeed.

The fear of losing keeps us from trying to win.

The fear of what everyone else will think keeps us from stepping out boldly.

The fear of ridicule keeps us from declaring our faith in Jesus Christ. Most of all, fear stifles hope.

There is a reason I am still here, and fear has no part in that. I know that God still has a purpose and a plan for me here on earth—to accomplish more with my life, and to share my faith with other people. That is one of the reasons I have written this book.

I hope that by sharing some of my life experiences and the lessons I've learned, I've given you hope. Hope from my heart to yours. And I also want to leave you with the best anti-fear medicine I know. It is the "spirit of hope" in Christ that overcomes the fears of the world.